Animals of the Night

T0018099

WOLVES
AFTER DARK

Heather M. Moore Niver

Enslow Publishing
101 W. 23rd Street
Suite 240
New York, NY 10011
USA

enslow.com

Words to Know

captivity—Kept in a cage or fence.

carnivores—Animals that eat only meat.

conservation—To protect or restore something to its natural surroundings.

endangered—In danger of no longer existing.

extinct—No longer existing.

jackal—Another wolf-like member of the dog family.

nocturnal—Mostly active at night.

pack—A group of animals, usually wild, that live together, such as coyotes or wolves.

predators—Animals that kill and eat other animals to stay alive.

prey—An animal hunted by another animal for food.

prowling—Moving about quietly and secretly.

Contents

Predator in the Night

In the dead of night, a wolf howls to call to its **pack**. The **prowling** wolf has a group of moose in sight. At the chilling sound of a wolf's hungry howl, the moose scatter. The pack closes in on the smallest, slowest animal. The **predators** put on a burst of speed and quickly surround their next meal. Then they all attack! The pack quickly takes down the moose. They all dig in. They eat until only bones and fur are left. Once full, the wolves relax a little. Another hunt has been a success for these **nocturnal** animals.

FUN FACT!

Wolves are smart and strong. American Indians named their greatest warriors after them. In stories, powerful characters are named after wolves.

Wolves have been respected for their size and their amazing hunting skills. They usually search for **prey** at night.

Gray, Red, and Ethiopian Wolves

Do you think wolves look a lot like large dogs? That is because they are part of the dog family. In fact, they are the largest of all the dogs, or canid family.

The gray wolf is also known as a timber wolf. It is the largest member of the family. Its fur is usually gray or a yellowish-brown tan. Some gray wolves may be reddish or almost black. Most male gray wolves weigh about 100 pounds (45 kilograms). They might be over 6 feet (2 meters) long, including their tails.

Gray wolves even have large paws. They can reach 4 inches (10 centimeters) across by 5 inches (almost 13 centimeters) long!

Red wolves are another type of wolf. They are not always red, though. Their fur is usually reddish brown or tan. It may also be yellow, black, or gray. No matter what color they are, most red wolves have some red fur. It is usually behind their legs or ears. Males usually weigh between 60 and 80 pounds (27 and 36 kg). They grow to be about 5 feet long (about 1 ½ m) long. That's about the size of a German shepherd dog.

FUN FACT!

In the 1970s, scientists thought the wild red wolf was **extinct**. They were able to raise some wolves in **captivity**. They introduced them to a safe place to live in North Carolina. About one hundred of them live there today.

Red wolves usually have some reddish fur on their bodies. They also have white legs.

The Ethiopian wolf was once considered a jackal. The jackal is another member of the dog family. Scientists later realized that this animal is related to gray wolves. It was larger and had longer legs than a jackal. Its fur is also more like the fur of a wolf. Ethiopian wolves have red fur and black and white tails. They have one white spot on their chests. They are the only kind of wolf in all of Africa. This small group goes by many other names: Abyssinian fox, red fox, red jackal, Simien fox, or Simien jackal.

FUN FACT!

Ethiopian wolves are the rarest wolves on the planet. Scientists judge that there may only be around five hundred of them living in Ethiopia. There are so few that they are endangered.

Ethiopian wolves are the only wolves that do not live in North America.

Top Dog

Wolves don't really have any natural enemies, except for humans. A healthy wolf can live for up to thirteen years in the wild. Most don't reach such an "old" age. They may die as a result of disease. Some areas have a high wolf population. There, wolves might be killed by other wolves. Or they might die of starvation.

More often, however, wolves die because of humans. Gray wolves were once heavily hunted. They were in danger of becoming extinct in the United States.

Humans are wolves' only real enemy. People hunted gray wolves until there were hardly any of them left.

Social Beasts

Usually, wolves like to live with other wolves in groups called packs. A pack is usually made up of two adult wolves and their offspring. The male and female adults are the leaders of the pack. They are called the alpha pair. They usually live in packs of between six and ten wolves. A pack can include up to twenty-four wolves.

Wolves usually hunt in packs. They do most of their hunting at night. The pack looks for a sick or weak animal in a herd. Then they surround it and attack it together.

FUN FACT!

Wolves have very strong jaws. They can bite through their prey's thick skin and break hard bones.

Wolves are social animals that usually live in packs.

Hungry!

Wolves have huge appetites. Some will eat up to 20 pounds (9 kg) of food at a time. Gray wolves are strict **carnivores**. They hunt large animals, such as moose, goats, sheep, and deer. The smaller red wolves dine on smaller prey. Their meals are made up of animals such as rabbits, rodents, and even insects. These wolves are a little less picky than gray wolves. Red wolves will sometimes snack on berries, too. Ethiopian wolves also hunt larger prey. Most of the time they fill up on rodents as well.

FUN FACT!

Wolves rarely attack humans, but if they have the chance, they will hunt household pets.

A pair of gray wolves feed on a large deer.

Have Paws, Will Travel

A gray wolf's body is designed to do a lot of traveling. It has a narrow chest. It also has long legs and large paws. These are the perfect shapes for covering long distances. Wolves can reach speeds of 37 miles (60 km) per hour. They use speed to catch prey.

Wolves may travel hundreds of miles from their home in search of food.

Wolves can travel up to 12 miles (20 km) in a single day. Most of their travel is at night. They like the night when it is cool. The darkness helps them avoid humans, too.

Howling and Other Communication

Wolves are famous for their howl. Howling is a great way to communicate. They howl over long distances and in the dark. One wolf might howl to get its pack's attention. Packs of wolves will howl to let others know where they are. Sometimes, wolves howl just to join in with the others. Dogs do this, too. Wolves also bark to communicate a warning. They whimper to let others know they give up. A mother whimpers to let her young know she will feed them milk. Growling is their way of sending a warning.

FUN FACT!

Wolves like to play by throwing things like bones and branches to each other!

Wolves might be howling to talk to the rest of their pack.

Sometimes wolves want to communicate silently. They let their pack know how they feel with body language. When they disagree, they bare their teeth. They also stick their ears up.

Wolves also use scent, such as in their urine, to mark places. This lets other wolves know they have been there. Wolves have a fantastic sense of smell. It is one hundred times more sensitive than ours. Wolves use their snouts to sniff out their next meal. Sometimes that sensitive nose knows when an enemy is near.

A wolf's sense of smell is much better than ours!

Hey, Baby!

When baby wolves are born, they are called pups. They only weigh about one pound (0.5 kg). A group of pups, called a litter, usually contains between four and six babies.

The pups' eyes are closed for the first eleven to fifteen days. Wolf pups hardly have any sense of smell  when they are born. The pups are also deaf. But they have a good sense of taste. They drink their mother's milk until they are ten weeks old. Then they can eat solid food.

FUN FACT!

The whole pack takes care of pups after they are born. Sometimes they bring them food. They might keep an eye on them when other pack members are out hunting.

A pup's eyes are blue when they first open. After two to four months, they change to a golden color.

Critical Conservation

At one time, there were many wolves around the world. They were almost as widespread as humans are today. They lived all across North America. They traveled from Alaska and Canada. Wolves were also in central Mexico. They lived in northern areas of Europe and Asia, too. Ancient people liked how the wolves could survive under tough conditions.

Modern humans have thought of wolves as evil and threatening. They felt the wolves competed for the same animals they wanted to hunt. They also didn't like that the wolves were hunting their farm animals.

Ancient people were impressed by
wolves' effective hunting. They tried
to copy their methods.

Back in the 1800s and 1900s, people felt threatened by wolves. They did everything they could to kill them. So by 1950, there was only a group left in Minnesota. Finally, in the later twentieth century, people spoke up to protect wolves. Now, the population is back up to 65,000–78,000 in North America. The wolf numbers are much better. However, they are still endangered. Wolves need our protection.

FUN FACT!

In the 1980s, biologists and other people were concerned about wolves. They started a special wolf project. It helped bring the gray wolf back to Yellowstone National Park.

Stay Safe Around Wolves

Wolves are mysterious and exciting animals. Seeing one in the wild would be amazing! But it's important to stay safe around these dangerous hunters.

 If a wolf comes toward you, don't run.

 Clap your hands, make noise, and step toward the wolf.

 Never turn your back on a wolf. Stare at it.

 If you are with another person, stand back to back with your friend. Move away from the wolves.

 Use sticks or rocks to scare off the wolves.

 Loud noises like horns might scare off a wolf.

 Wolves cannot climb. Climb a tree if there is no other option.

Learn More

Books

Gangemi, Alphia. *Hunting Wth Wolves*. New York: Gareth Stevens Publishing, 2012.

Llanas, Sheila Griffin. *Gray Wolves*. Minneapolis: Abdo Publishers, 2013.

Marsh, Laura F. *Wolves*. Washington, DC: National Geographic, 2012.

Meinking, Mary. *Wolf vs. Elk*. Chicago: Raintree, 2011.

Websites

Ducksters: Red Wolf
ducksters.com/animals/red_wolf.php
Learn more about red wolves with facts, photos, and information about how and why they are endangered.

National Geographic Kids: Gray Wolf
kids.nationalgeographic.com/animals/gray-wolf
Maps, facts, and photos tell the story of the gray wolf.

Wolf Conservation Center
nywolf.org
Watch live wolf video-cams, listen to wolf calls, and learn how you can help keep the wolf population healthy.

Index

To Zoe, my wild and wondrous Wolf Girl

Published in 2016 by Enslow Publishing, LLC
101 W. 23rd Street, Suite 240, New York, NY 10011

Copyright © 2016 by Enslow Publishing, LLC.

Library of Congress Cataloging-in-Publication Data

Niver, Heather Moore, author.
 Wolves after dark / Heather M. Moore Niver.
    pages cm. — (Animals of the night)
Audience: Ages 8+
Audience: Grades 4 to 6
 Summary: "Describes the habits and nature of wolves at night"—
Provided by publisher.
 Includes bibliographical references and index.
 ISBN 978-0-7660-7418-7 (library binding)
 ISBN 978-0-7660-7416-3 (pbk)
 ISBN 978-0-7660-7417-0 (6-pack)
1. Wolves—Behavior—Juvenile literature. 2. Wolves—Juvenile
literature. I. Title.
 QL737.C22N585 2016
 599.773—dc23

                        2015026945

Printed in the United States of America

To Our Readers: We have done our best to make sure all website addresses in this book were active and appropriate when we went to press. However, the author and the publisher have no control over and assume no liability for the material available on those websites or on any websites they may link to. Any comments or suggestions can be sent by e-mail to customerservice@enslow.com.hotos

Photo Credits: Throughout book, narvikk/E+/Getty Images (starry background), kimberrywood/Digital Vision Vectors/Getty Images (green moon dingbat); cover, p. 1 Olga_i/Shutterstock.com, samxmed/E+/Getty Images (moon); p. 3 Chad Graham/Moment/Getty Images; p. 5 Art Wofle/iconica/Getty Images; p. 7 Denis Pepin/Shutterstock.com; p. 9 Mark Conlin/Oxford Scientific/Getty Images; p. 11 © Shah, Anup/Animals Animals—Earth Scenes; p. 13 Tom Tietz/Shutterstock.com; p. 15 © Michael Cummings/Moment/Getty Images; p. 17 Lori Labrecque/Shutterstock.com; pp. 18–19 Patrick Endres/Design Pics/First Light/Getty Images; p. 21 Jupiterimages/Photos.com/Thinkstock; p. 23 nialat/Shutterstock.com; p. 25 Jim and Jamie Dutcher/National Geographic/Getty Images; p. 27 Sergia Pitamitz/National Geographic/Getty Images; p. 29 Greg Toope/Shutterstock.com.